Empath

Understanding Your Gift,
Protecting your Energy and
Finding Peace in a Chaotic World

Jessica Greiner

including specific information will be considered an illegal act irrespective of if it is done electronically or in print. This extends to creating a secondary or tertiary copy of the work or a recorded copy and is only allowed with an express written consent from the Publisher. All additional right reserved.

The information in the following pages is broadly considered to be a truthful and accurate account of facts, and as such any inattention, use or misuse of the information in question by the reader will render any resulting actions solely under their purview. There are no scenarios in which the publisher or the original author of this work can be in any fashion deemed liable for any hardship or damages that may befall them after undertaking information described herein.

Additionally, the information in the following pages is intended only for informational purposes and should thus be thought of as universal. As befitting its nature, it is presented without assurance regarding its prolonged validity or interim quality. Trademarks that are mentioned are done without written consent and can in no way be considered an endorsement from the trademark holder.

This book is designed to provide accurate and authoritative information in regard to the subject matter covered. By its sale, neither the publisher nor the author is engaged in rendering psychological or other professional services. If expert assistance or counseling is needed, the services of a competent professional should be sought.

Table of Contents

Introduction

Congratulations on choosing *Empath: Understanding Your Gift, Protecting your Energy and Finding Peace in a Chaotic World*, and thank you for doing so.

Have you ever walked into a room and felt an immediate rush of overwhelming emotions? When meeting new people, do you often feel specific vibes that tell you everything you need to know about a person? What about your interpersonal relationships? Do people tend to dump their problems on you on a regular basis? Do you often feel drained after associating with certain people or even attending social events? If you have ever felt these emotions before, you have probably been diagnosed with some form of social anxiety. However, there is a rare gift that only impacts about 5% of the population.

This gift mimics the signs of anxiety but is met with natural abilities far beyond the scope of fear. If you have ever experienced the pain of someone else to the point where it's become your own, you may be what psychologists call an Empath or highly sensitive person. Science has made tremendous strides with raising awareness on the medical and scientific legitimacy of this notion. Countless research studies, books, and even private practices are dedicated to researching more into the mind of an Empathic person. This absorption of emotions is quite mysterious, yet tantalizing in its complexity.

Although paralyzed by the stigma of this society, sensitivity isn't a sign of overwhelming weakness. Many children deemed sensitive may face bullying in school. Highly emotional people in the workplace may be passed for opportunities. However, despite how society views the outward display of emotions, being in tune with the emotions of others is something beautiful. In fact, it is a mark of the brave. A sign of the compassionate. It is something to be valued. Being able to read people through behavior, energy, and vibrations is something unique that should be taken seriously.

Living in a chaotic world, however, it may be quite difficult to see beauty insensitivity. The running trend in this society is to be tough and lack care for others. You may deal with unhealthy relationships and even confusion as a result of your gift. Therefore, you need a guidebook to finding your balance despite feelings of intense Empathy. Creating a universe of support for yourself is essential.

How can you manage your sanity and create meaningful relationships? Are there key secrets to finding your purpose? How can you manage perfectionism when others don't seem to live up to your expectations? Is there a way to keep the emotions I am feeling in their place without compromising my ability? Can I embrace my gift with confidence? All of these questions and many more will be answered throughout this book. By taking in the information written, you will see that high sensitivity isn't a paranormal or mythical feeling shared by magical creatures. Rather, it is a scientific diagnosis that rings with compassion, strength, and kindness.

There are plenty of books on this subject on the market, thanks again for choosing this one! Every effort was made to ensure it is full of as much useful information as possible; please enjoy!

Chapter 1:
Empath - More than Just a Fictional Superpower

The word *Empath* has sparked heightened curiosity for millions of individuals worldwide, seeking to understand their emotions further. Countless spiritual advisors proclaim the legitimacy of Empathic abilities through YouTube channels, books, and group workshops. Guru's make millions of dollars annually by proclaiming to feel the emotions of another. They use these gifts as a mean to solicit advice, at a cost. In fact, the term "spiritual business" has been coined to categorize this line of work. Despite speculation surrounding the accuracy of Empathic abilities, many knowledge seekers are self-diagnosing themselves as Empaths. The mystery surrounding this heightened sense of sensitivity is intriguing. However, are Empathic abilities more than just a paranormal superpower to enhance books and movies?

The dictionary definition of an Empath is, "(*chiefly in science fiction*) a person with the paranormal ability to apprehend the mental or emotional state of another individual." Another source defined Empath as, "taking on the emotions of others." One popular author Christel

Chapter 1: Empath - More than Just a Fictional Superpower

Broederlow says, "Empaths often possess the ability to sense others on many different levels," this includes the abilities to understand what a person desires intimately, yearns for, and is currently feeling, suffering or thinking, as well as the ability to feel other people's bodily illnesses. These occurrences manifest themselves as energy vibrations that the finely tuned Empath can pick up on, or "tune into."

Empaths experience the pain, anxiety, and distress of those around them. They even experience discomfort associated with nature and animals. Their senses are heightened to levels beyond simple understanding. Imagine walking into a room and feeling the physical sensation of the movements, emotions, and dispositions of those around. Sure, everyone has experienced some situation where Empathy was required. However, being an Empath encompasses something far deeper than understanding how someone else feels.

Empath Characteristics include:

- The ability to feel the physical and emotional distress of someone else.

- An intense disdain for violent or depressing entertainment.

- A strong, intuitive feeling about another person without even knowing them.

- The ability to see through deception, lack of sincerity, and ulterior motives in others.

- Not finding pleasure or enjoyment in crowds or public places.

- Compassionate listening and a trustworthy demeanor.

- Deeply affected by the emotional distress
  of others.

- Connected to the arts, creativity, animals,
  and nature.

Highly sensitive individuals are also prone to
feeling the energy of food. They often have
nutritional and dietary restrictions due to their
sensitive digestive system. These sensitivities
aren't limited to consuming certain foods. Highly
sensitive individuals are also extremely sensitive
to loud noises, extreme temperatures, and even
bright lights.

The average person can experience Empathy
when witnessing the sadness or disappointment
of another person. At the moment, they are
affected, but that feeling soon goes away. The
difference between traditional Empathy and an
Empath is the ability to separate one person's
feelings from their own. They can feel the

emotions of the people the around, and that in turn, drains their energy. They may be deeply affected by their surroundings, and this impacts their function. Empaths experience compassion, Empathy, care, and worry on a heightened level.

Empaths Experience Heightened Intuition

Intuition can be likened to a feeling directed at a person, situation, or future event. Often, individuals have an unspoken and unidentifiable means of acquiring information regarding a person, for example, by simply looking at them. This intuitiveness guides their behavior so much so; they can decide whether to pursue a relationship or move on. Empathic people have a strong connection with their intuition that provides them with the ability to read others. This awareness goes beyond determining if someone is trustworthy or dangerous. This skill allows Empathic people the ability to determine someone's future, past, and immediate experiences.

Although often confused with psychic, or paranormal powers, Empaths can read energy sources through vibrations. For example, a traditional Empath has the ability to pick up on a person's energy and determine their anxiety, pain, and discomfort levels through close contact. If someone had a stressful day at work, an Empath could sense that intensity. In turn, they can offer realistic advice as they are physically able to feel another's pain. In fact, Empaths have been known to take on the worries of others so much; they become physically drained in the process. Also, Empaths are increasingly difficult to double cross. Since they have the heightened ability to read others, they can sense fraudulent or insincere motives. This is partly why they are often associated with being introverted or shy. Empaths who lack understanding of their feelings may experience depression, anxiety, even anger because they are not fully aware of their sensitivities.

When humans internalize their emotions, often they display signs of distress that the typical person wouldn't notice. For example, stress can cause the body to curl inward. Slight sways, twitches, and even tone of voice can indicate anxiety. To the untrained eye, one may dismiss the anxious individual's signals. Empaths, on the other hand, can pick up on that negative energy so heavily, they begin to experience feelings of distress. These may even induce panic or anxiety attacks. When carrying a conversation with an Empath, they directly analyze the tone and words their householder is using to make an inference on that person's emotions and intentions.

A highly sensitive person is guided by their intuition to read others. They can meet someone and immediately know if they are trustworthy or pure at heart. The signs differ from one Empath to the other, but they all make a concise decision based on a feeling. Some may like this to a hunch or an inkling. They can pay attention to small social cues that may not be as visible to the non-Empath eye. Unfortunately, sociopaths and narcissists are drawn to Empaths because they are so good at hiding their true intentions and can take advantage of the situation.

Empaths allegedly can feel the emotions of others even when separated. For example, if an Empaths friend or family member experiences a traumatic situation, the Empath may be able to feel their pain even miles away despite not being aware of the current distress. While this specific trait has not been proven scientifically, many Empaths have reported situations similar to those above.

Another alleged gift is the ability to feel the earth's distress. Some Empathic people reportedly can feel when hurricanes, earthquakes, and even tsunamis are about to occur. They rely on the energy force that permeates through the earth as a guidepost to their feelings. Similar to the example listed above, science has not officially proven the validity of these remarks.

When entering crowded areas, the intensity of multiple emotions can prove to be paralyzing for the Empath. This impacts the Empaths ability to focus and even enjoy crowded areas. They report feeling drained and a drastic loss of energy. Imagine taking on the joy, sadness, anxiety, fatigue, or the excitement of multiple individuals at once. Surely, calling it overwhelming would be underestimating the situation regarding explaining it. Corporate and large office environments are detrimental to an Empaths happiness and productivity. Since they prefer to communicate digitally, in-person interactions are extremely dissatisfying, especially when having to engage in small talk. Many Empaths find success working from home, freelancing, or pursuing creative careers that don't require a pressured structure or constant face to face interaction.

Although sometimes draining, Empaths are drawn to careers that involve care-taking or guiding others. Such jobs include teachers, counselors, nurses, and even artists. Since Empaths have such a strong connection with nature and the arts, they strive in creative environments that allow them the ability to express their emotions freely. Police investigators and detectives may often use Empaths to assist with crime scenes. Since they have the ability to read others and detect discrepancies, their intuitiveness is useful for discovering detailed information.

The Downfall of Being an Empath

Unfortunately, constant intuitiveness to the stressors of the world can leave Empathic individuals drained. Since their biological and neurological makeup absorbs outward emotions on a grand scale, many suffer from physical health problems. Severe depression and consistent anxiety are the most common side effects. Digestive issues, back pain, and headaches are also prevalent in Empathic individuals. Being exposed to stress on such a consistent basis makes for a weak immune system and even chronic fatigue.

Socially, Empathic individuals are compassionate. Therefore, others are naturally drawn to their trustworthy demeanor. Unfortunately, this causes Empaths to be taken advantage of emotionally. Narcissists, sociopaths, and other manipulative individuals use Empaths as prey. One writer denotes, "Since sociopaths don't have emotions they don't feel whole within themselves. There is a gaping hole inside, and they want to have the emotions that others have to fill it. They want to feel love. They want to feel sadness and happiness too. So, when the sociopath spots the Empath, they usually find themselves attracted. I think this is because they instinctively know they need whatever the Empath has. They start their manipulation by luring the Empath in. They use body language, mannerisms, subtle gestures, eye contact, etc. to lure the Empath in. And, Empaths are unfortunately suckers for this because of their attraction to the quiet, special feeling."

Often, making personal choices is difficult, mainly because Empaths are so focused on the emotions of others. They worry consistently about how their decisions may impact the opinions of those around them. This forces them to conform to an image of perfectionism. They may find a dissonance between wanting to please others and pleasing themselves. Seeking perfectionism in an attempt to appease others is a constant struggle.

Empaths are intuitive individuals when it comes to reading others. However, understanding their vulnerabilities may be a struggle. They may experience confusion with their own emotions that paralyze their confidence. They may battle with identifying the true source of their current mood. Is it their personal anxiety periling them, or is it someone around them? To cope with the overwhelming sensation of emotions surrounding them, many turns to harmful coping mechanisms like alcohol or drugs as an escape. Since they are so in tune with emotions, Empaths are also mistaken for being weak or overly sensitive which can impact their esteem. Moreover, this intense reaction to sensitive stimulants prevents them from finding enjoyment in violent or graphic entertainment. They tend to shun news or media platforms that discuss the injustices, cruelties, or misfortune occurring.

Empaths in Popular Culture

The connection between humans is powerful, yet mysterious. Popular culture feeds images of sociopaths or psychopaths as a means to entertain. The true spirit of these individuals is often tainted with media portrayal. Empaths are generally defined as the vigilante of humankind. The ones are so drastically different in behavior from an otherwise evil character that is positioned only to carry out good. With the help of medically trained professionals and curious researchers, the concept of being an Empath has evolved from something absurd and romanticized to a recognized characteristic. In fact, popular culture has taken the term Empath and turned it into an entire movement. Apparel, support groups, and even commercialized television shows speak freely on Empathic abilities. In fact, in 1968, a popular episode of *Star Trek* introduced the concept of Empath to the masses. The crew meets a new intergalactic species that has the power to absorb the pain felt by others. Although science fiction in nature, the concept of an ever feeling being living in a world of carelessness is something Empaths have to juggle on a daily basis.

Countless online tests have been established for individuals to self-diagnose themselves as being Empathic. One, in particular, probes test takers to rate themselves on a sliding scale of five options. One, strongly disagreeing with five being strongly agreed. Some questions include, "do you often feel the pain of others?", "you feel the same sensation or emotion around a specific person," "you feel physically or emotionally ill when seeing violent images in movies or on TV." After completion, the results will determine your Empathic diagnosis along with a specific symbolic animal that is used to represent your spirit. The process may seem amateur initially, but the written results are quite accurate when considered honestly. There are established facilities which focus primarily on Empathic individuals and they even test for high sensitivity. Many therapists and counselors also specialize in guiding highly sensitive individuals through the challenges of life.

The History of Empathy

Empathy is a relatively new concept that came from the word Einfühlung which means "feeling-in" in German. In 1908, the English term *Empathy* was derived from the Greek linguistics "em" and "pathos" which when translated means, in feeling. The exact definition of Empathy was still in its early stages. Psychologists were still seeking to connect Empathy to human nature properly. Empathy was not thought to be an abstract ability to feel others experiences. Rather, they took the definition literally and attributed Empathy to physically feeling the sensation of thoughts or objects through thought.

They believed a person could physically feel the properties, texture, and attributes of anything they imagined. For example, one study was told to recall a vine of grapes and describe his feelings. He reported, "A cool, juicy feeling all over. A feeling of smoothness and softness all over me."[1] Over 40 years later, psychologist Rosalind Cartwright sought to transform the previous notion of Empathy and give it a social makeover. Through decades of multiple studies

---

[1] Dallenbach, K.M., Bentley, M., Garrigues, E., Washburn, M.F. (1910). The American Journal of Psychology p.448

focusing on how emotions can be aroused through the experiences of others, psychologist C. Daniel Batson can be credited for defining Empathy as it is commonly known today. Through a combination of personal research in conjunction with the pioneers of psychology mentioned earlier, he developed eight concepts of Empathy. According to the Association for Psychological Science, those eight concepts include[2]:

1. Knowing another thoughts and feelings

2. Imagining another's thoughts and feelings.

3. Adopting the posture of another.

4. Actually feeling as another does.

---

[2] The Atlantic. (2015). Association for Psychological Science. The Atlantic-A Short History of Empathy. Available at: https://www.theatlantic.com/health/archive/2015/10/a-short-history-of-empathy/409912/

5. Imagining how one would feel or think in another's place.

6. Feeling distressed at another's suffering.

7. Feeling for another's suffering.

8. Projecting oneself into another's situation.

What Empaths and Highly Sensitive People Are Not

Overstimulation and sensitivity to certain foods are similar characteristics of Autism. While the traits may coincide, the developmental structure of the two is drastically different. One, being highly sensitive is not a recognized "*disorder*." The effects of being highly sensitive can mirror anxiety, bipolar disorder, and even depression. However, you are not going to find Empath on the list of official human behavior disorders. Empathic individuals have also been confused with introverts. While they find peace in solitude, they aren't afraid of crowds. They enjoy being around others. They are capable of engaging in social events.

However, they simply have a limit to their fun, and that's when they need to retreat to recharge. Also, being an Empath does not mean a person has psychic or paranormal abilities. They cannot foretell the future nor do they possess telepathic abilities. The appeal of holistic and energy centering exercises, however, is naturally drawn to Empathic people. The spiritual experience is something of importance to them. This creates a community of people with proclaimed clairvoyant abilities. As we discuss the science behind HSP (high sensitive people) more, you will understand the neurology behind these individuals. We will also refer to Empaths as highly sensitive people throughout the duration of this e-book.

Empath

Empaths, in general, are grouped in a category of alternative and metaphysical abilities. When researching *Empath*, one may find sources that tap into spiritual or paranormal outlets. Although many spirit mediums claim to have clairvoyant or physic abilities, the diagnosis of being an Empath is scientifically legitimate and backed by measurable qualities. Although associated with the spirit realm, this book focuses solely on scientific backing along with practical tools for Empaths to utilize in their daily lives. Now that the word Empath has been clearly defined let's consider the neurological and scientific proof behind Empathic or highly sensitive abilities.

Chapter 2:
The Science behind Empathy

Physics suggests that energy can come in various uses. Kinetic energy controls motion which ascribes to environmental or solar energy sources such as lightning, waves, and temperature. In fact, one snowflake falling can generate 650 units of kinetic energy.[3] Over a century ago, innovator Nikola Tesla stated, "The day science begins to study non-physical phenomena, and it will make more progress in one decade than in all the previous centuries of its existence. To understand the true nature of the universe, one must think regarding energy, frequency, and vibration."

---

[3] Elert, G. (2018). The Physics Hypertext Book. Available at:
https://physics.info/

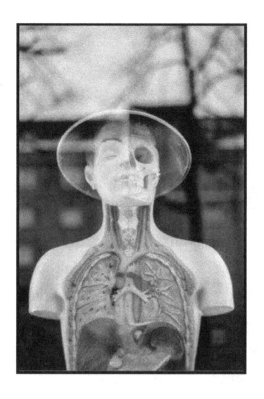

Science is now embracing the fact that measurable components can have an impact on the things unseen. The energy we release physically has a lot to do with our mental state of mind. Everything in the universe contains a specific energy field and vibration. From trees to animals, to newborn infants, we all release a specific energy field. When it comes to humans, energy can be defined in both an abstract and measurable manner.

The practice of neuroscience strives to break boundaries with this theory. The conscious state of a person's mind, containing his thoughts, memories, experience, and behavior can rebuild matter which is essentially energy. In essence, our conscious awareness can directly impact the energy we release. This directly affects mood, body posture, disposition, and speech. Often, when experiencing a great deal of stress, many report others noticing a change of tone in their voice. This may attribute to a mother speaking with her daughter over the phone and hearing the distress in her voice, even without knowing the problem at hand.

The human energy field is complex yet astounding. The visible work of tissues and cells can be measured through electrical fields that even appear on the skin.[4] Being that the nervous system works in conjunction with all areas of the body, the mood can directly alter the production of certain cells and hormones, and impact recovery from diseases. No wonder certain emotions are manifested into physical signals like smiling for happiness. When it comes to displaying cues that signal certain emotions, Empaths can pick up on the subtle energy being released. This can be attributed to electromagnetic fields being released from the brain and the heart. These fields may easily be detected by Empaths which causes them to pick up on the emotions of others. Empaths are sensitive to the output of energy which makes them ideal for medical careers.

Neuroscience has made tremendous strides in researching the different functions of brain cells.

---

[4] Oschman, N., Oschman, J. (2018). Reiki News Articles. The International Center for Reiki Training. Science Measures the Human Energy Field. Available at: http://www.reiki.org/reikinews/sciencemeasures.htm

Chapter 2: The Science behind Empathy

A recent study conducted by researchers Max Planck and Tania Singer[5] showcased how various emotions affect brain function. There is a section of the brain called the supramarginal gyrus located in the cerebral cortex which essentially controls compassion and Empathy. In their published study found in the *Journal of Neuroscience*, the curious researchers studied the right supramarginal gyrus which is located near the front of the brain. This controls one's ability to pick up on when Empathy is needed and to detect when someone isn't showing it. In groups of two, the researchers presented two tangible options for the participants to examine. One was told to grasp slime while looking at a picture of maggots while the other was given faux fur and a photo of a puppy. Ironically, the two participants were able to see the others reaction.

---

[5] Bergland, C. (2013). Psychology Today. The Neuroscience of Empathy. Available at: https://www.psychologytoday.com/intl/blog/the-athletes-way/201310/the-neuroscience-empathy

After the exposure, the group was instructed to express their reaction or emotion to the stimulus in comparison to what their partner received. The one who was given the photo of the puppy felt that the reaction of their partner, who was given the slime and maggots, was dramatic. Since they had a great experience, those emotions clouded the individual's perception to understand what his partner was going through. In addition, the opposing partner who underwent a negative experience didn't feel as if his partner's experience was all that great. This study concluded that individuals could only experience true Empathy if they share similar experiences. This is where the right supramarginal gyrus comes into action to redirect selfish thinking and replace it with compassion.

It is safe to conclude that those participants were not Empaths. However, this study can assist with understanding the neurological makeup of Empathic or highly sensitive people. Perhaps brain activity that takes place within the cerebral cortex is more active in Empaths. Researchers who study psychopaths found that when exposed to images of pain being inflicted on others, the ventral striatum, which handles pleasure, was heightened. If science can prove the validity of an extreme lack of Empathy, it is only accurate that it can prove the validity of Empaths.

Mirror Neurons and Emotional Contagion

The running theme surrounding Empaths and highly sensitive individuals is the presence of overactive brain cells that contribute to their abilities to respond to sensory stimulants on a heightened level. Mirror neurons are tiny cells located in the brain that handle emotions. However, mirror neurons are unique in that they allow individuals the capability to feel the pain of others. This could be the reason why funerals

Empath

spark emotions in individuals who didn't know the deceased. By seeing other people cry, they cry. Empaths may have mirror neurons that operate on a higher level than non-Empaths. This sensitivity gives them the unique ability to not only understand the emotions of others but feel them.[6]

Emotional contagion is a theory that suggests one mood change can interrupt the mood of everyone else. For instance, an angry boss can essential "dampen the mood" of the entire office by demonstrating aggressive behavior. This can impact productivity within the entire office as others are now feeling on edge. In contrast, one who lacks Empathy may brush off their boss's behavior and continue to work. Empaths can distinguish between outright displays of emotion and subtle clues.

---

[6] Orloff, J. (2017). Psychology Today. The Science behind Empathy and Empaths. Available at: https://www.psychologytoday.com/intl/blog/the-empaths-survival-guide/201703/the-science-behind-empathy-and-empaths

Chapter 2: The Science behind Empathy

The theory of Perspective Taking has four different levels that surround perception, vantage point, and overall Empathy. At the basic level, a person understands that others are different and have opposing views or experiences. Empaths encompass all four levels simultaneously, but they excel at level three which includes mirroring another person's emotions. Here, they can visualize, feel, and understand the thoughts of someone else.

In summation, it's proven that humans give off unique energy that is directly impacted by moods, thoughts, and experiences. When having a stressful day, the vibrations being released have a specific "*code*" that Empaths can pick up on. Since they have heightened brain cells and function that operate on a sensitive level, this gives them the ability to not only detect those emotions but feel them as well. Perhaps Empaths are a combination of neurological, social, and psychological components that increase their perception. Thus far, the information covered has given scientific and social definitions of the word Empath. Do these characteristics resonate with you? Could you perhaps be an Empath or highly sensitive person? If so, the following chapters will discuss practical advice on honing in on your ability and developing useful tools to navigate the world.

Chapter 3:
Essential Tools for Managing the Struggles of High Sensitivity

Many believe that being a sensitive person automatically equates weakness. Often, when you visually display your emotions, you are assumed to be weak. Since Empaths essentially absorb the feelings of others, they are a cannonball of emotions that are overwhelming. Do you often feel the pain of others so intensely that it drives you to tears? If so, understand that being sensitive does not mean you are a weak person. Being an Empath, you can experience Empathy so deeply, your compassion shows. By understanding your gift, this will assist you with redefining sensitivity as something unique.

Breaking the Stigma behind Sensitivity

Some synonyms for sensitive are responsive, cognizant, perceptive, and conscious. All terms that require knowledge and dignity. Sure, the world may see you as tense or emotional, but that's okay. Taking on the burden of changing the perspectives of an entire society is vast and virtually impossible. However, focus then on what you can control. Your perspective.

When you begin to view Empathic abilities as something unique, you will no longer fight them. Sensitivity is defined as, "quick to detect or respond to slight changes, signals, or influences." Did you see the words *weak*, *fragile*, or *lowly*? Highly sensitive people can perceive signals and changes in the personalities of others in a heightened manner. Often the way one responds to their sensitivities may appear weak or timid to the untrained eye. Despite how others perceive your gift, you have to see past the ignorance to become empowered. You can change the way you see yourself through a series of daily exercises.

Practicing Mindfulness

Practicing mindfulness is extremely calming and effective. Mindfulness can be defined as engaging the moment without seeking to control it. You are permitting yourself to feel at peace despite the chaos. How can you make mindfulness a daily habit? Practicing deep breathing exercises is one beneficial way. Position yourself in a calm and quiet environment that is free from distraction. Concentrate on your breathing and try your best to block out your thoughts and emotions. Deep breathe in and feel your belly expand. Exhale slowly, and relax. Repeating this exercise daily will help you to center your energy and focus on yourself. When you focus your attention on what you can control, the overwhelming emotions of others will become manageable.

Empaths are selfless people, and they put the needs of others above their own. This mindset is awesome and truly what the world needs. Despite the honor, the world is imperfect and full of evil. The importance of establishing your self-worth will help you to avoid negative people and situations. You will know how to separate

Individuals who experience a great deal of anxiety allow themselves to feel the anxiety without attempting to manipulate it. This can be difficult for Empaths because they not only have to manage their own emotions, but they also take on the feelings of others. Even so, sit in that uncomfortable place until you grow a tolerance. Understand that you cannot control the emotions of others, but you can control your response to them. By making your mind a safe place, you will conquer feeling drained.

Practice Self-Affirmations

Empaths are generally pleasers. They want to appeal to the hearts of those around them. Often, this mentality can blind an Empath to their desires. Thus, they are more susceptible to feelings of low self-worth. As mentioned, many Empaths turn to unhealthy coping mechanisms in effect to deal with the surplus of emotions they experience. In order to combat those feelings of worthlessness, self-affirmations are key.

To control your mood and heighten your energy, you have to build a strong sense of self. By forcing yourself to write down or repeat your strengths on a daily basis, the temptation to succumb to negative thinking will dwindle. Begin by talking about your strengths. Surely, compassion is one of them. Do not allow your ability to feel intensely spark negative emotions. Rather, take what you or others consider a weakness, and turn it into a positive. By documenting these traits daily, you'll begin to grow stronger with your sense of self.

Understand Your Trigger Points

As an Empath, you understand how violent movies, television shows, and even music can impact your overall mood. Often, watching the news can cause intense feelings of sadness that can linger for days. Exposing yourself to media outlets that cause anxiety simply to make those around you comfortable is counterproductive to your health. Sure, they may not completely understand nor initially believe the degree of your sensitivity. Therefore, open communication is essential. Explain to them how impactful violent or depressing entertainment is not only on your mental health but your physical as well.

Suggest alternative means of entertainment that won't affect your mood. This doesn't encourage living a sheltered life. Some exposure can diffuse being naive. It's important to understand what you can, and cannot handle. After establishing your boundaries, make an effort to stick to them despite fearing what others may think.

Embrace Holistic Options for Energy Cleansing

As an Empath, you are likely drawn to remedies of the earth. Fortunately, alternative means of healing are now being offered at commercial stores making the search for holistic options easier. There are a variety of relaxing methods that can accompany your lifestyle and restore your energy. Salt is an awesome tool for removing negativity and restoration. Specifically, Himalayan salt lamps release negative ions that cleanse the body, mind, and environment. By placing salt in your bath water, you can also receive the restoring benefits while forcing your body to relax. In addition, essential oils have proven properties that help to alleviate stress, increase energy, and promote mental clarity. Some include:

- Lavender and Chamomile for anxiety, peaceful sleep, and immunity.

- Ginger, Lemon, Eucalyptus for improved energy levels.

- Tea tree oil, Rosemary, and Sage to ward off harmful chemicals, treat wounds, and promote healing from physical distress.[7]

Oils derived from herbs and flowers have a unique makeup that can assist with mood and immunity. You can place these oils in a diffuser, bath, or mix them with lotion. It's imperative though, to consult with your doctor or healthcare provider before topically applying these oils. The

---

[7] Body Quirks. (2012). Total Body Solutions. Must Have Tools for the Empath. Available at: http://www.bodyquirks.com/2012/02/7-must-have-tools-for-the-empath/

properties of some may cause rashes, burns, or scare when used incorrectly.

Along with adding physical objects to restore energy, it's important to make your home a haven. Lighting candles, burning incense, and adding plants to your bedroom will help to enhance relaxation. By doing so, you have a "happy place" where you can go and recharge after a long day. This space should reflect positivity and energy boosting stimulants.

Schedule Alone Time and Understand Your Limit

In your past, you were likely confused when attempting to decode your emotions. You probably had no clue why you felt drained around certain people, noises, and crowds. Perhaps you even lost friendships because of this lack of understanding. Now that you understand why your reactions to others are so severe, you can create a mental *self-care* pact with yourself. Next time you are in a large group, document when you have reached your social limit. If it's two hours in, make a mental note and take action.

Don't stay around due to the obligation or the fear of offending others. It's time you put your emotional clarity in the forefront of your life. Now that you know your limit, you can implement that into your future social outings. If you must stay past your limit, find a safe space and go there. Many Empaths find solace by taking a few minutes in the bathroom, stepping outside, or relaxing in their car. By doing so, you are making your happiness a priority. Practice deep breathing, and center yourself so you can return energized.

One of the primary reasons why Empaths feel so comfortable in nature is because flowers, grass, trees, and the sun, don't drain their energy.

Empath

Instead, these elements energize the Empath while providing a relaxing environment for meditation. It's important to set aside time to embrace what nature has to offer you in order to recharge your batteries, so to speak. Science is now open to the idea that being around and touching trees can greatly impact mental and physical health. As mentioned, Empaths react to specific vibrations. This reaction could be positive or negative.

Trees release a unique vibration that is quite beneficial to regulating mental clarity, restoring energy, and balance. To prove this, researchers studied a group of children and placed them in an environment full of trees, plants, and flowers. Through this study, researchers found that when the children physically touched the elements of nature surrounding them, they were more creative, experienced improved behavior, and were less stressed.[8]

Pay Attention to Your Diet

As an Empath, you understand how susceptible you are to sickness, anxiety, and depression. Interacting with others may leave you drained which could cause chronic fatigue. A persistent presence of stress can alter the body's ability to defend against sickness. This causes a weak immune system among humans. Therefore, if an Empath is around a person with a cold, they will likely catch that sickness.

The importance of being mindful of what you are eating can work wonders for your physical and mental well-being. Probiotics that cleanse the digestive system will work wonders for stomach issues, acid reflux, and irritable bowel syndrome.

---

[8] The Mind Unleashed. (2013). Tree Hugging Now Scientifically Validated. Available at: https://themindunleashed.com/2013/07/tree-hugging-now-scientifically.html

Avoiding processed or foods saturated in fats will assist with chronic fatigue. Organic, leafy fruits and vegetables are known to boost energy levels naturally. By consuming foods in their natural state, free from harmful chemicals, you are allowing positive energy into your body.

Since animals give off energy fields and vibrations, many Empaths avoid eating meat. The manner in which the animal was killed could have a drastic impact on the Empaths ability to eat meat without feeling guilty. Some have reportedly been able to feel the negative energy of the animal which prompted them to take the vegetarian route.[9]

Embrace Creativity and Create

Empaths are naturally drawn to the arts and creativity as a whole. The process of painting,

---

[9] The Mind Unleashed. (2013). 30 Traits of the Empath. Available at: https://themindunleashed.com/2013/10/30-traits-of-empath.html

drawing, and even dancing is quite therapeutic. Living as an Empath, you are accustomed to taking in so many emotions on a daily basis. Likely, these emotions can be confusing and overwhelming.

You want to save the world from its menacing perils, but while that goal may be admirable, it's impossible. Expressing yourself through the arts can be a great means of purging that negative energy and creating something magnificent. Something you can control. This could alleviate the frustration surrounding not being able to fix everything. Surely, because the arts are meant to your soul, you are probably a natural creator.

Being an Empath requires a certain amount of time focused on restoring your energy. Although the burden of carrying a vast amount of emotions is weighty, you can conquer it! Making time for self-cleaning and healing will help you to remain balanced. You won't view your gift as something overwhelming. Rather, when you keep it in its proper place by making the time to build your strength, you are now in control. In addition, you have the mental strength to avoid pitfalls and being taken advantage of.

Now that you have your toolkit of restoration let's further analyze how being an Empath directly impacts your relationships. Social interactions are the primary source of drained energy and the absorption of unwanted emotions. Are there tips and tricks for navigating relationships without feeling drained?

Chapter 4:
Keeping Your Sanity - How to Reach Satisfaction in Your Relationships

Empaths often put everything into their relationships. This may cause their partners and friends to misunderstand their true intentions. They may view their Empathic friend as being needy, overly emotional, lacking independence, and even selfish. This lack of understanding can directly impact the value of interpersonal relationships. Many Empaths have been known to thrive in solitude; away from the noises and energy vampires of the world.

Empath

While it's necessary to schedule a proper alone time to recharge, the importance of developing meaningful relationships is vital. Since Empaths care deeply and feel intensely, their sanity is precious. Have you ever battled with your inner voice telling you to set reasonable boundaries, while your compassionate, Empathic abilities dominated the conversation? If so, likely you struggle with keeping your personal balance at bay. If so, consider four awesome tips to cultivate in order to remain sane when dealing with others.

Embrace Your Independence

"If I don't manage to fly, someone else will. The spirit wants only that there be flying. As for who happens to do it, in that he has only a passing interest." **Rainer Maria Rilke**.

This quote may resonate with you personally. Empaths have a strong desire to be free from the clutter of the world. Daily, you are consumed with distress from media outlets and personal interactions. The quote speaks about pulling yourself up and learning to fly on your own. This mentality may seem foreign to highly sensitive people because they are so used to helping others fly. The phrase, *"you cannot give from an empty cup"* is authentic and applicable. If you are not properly charged and independent, how can you expect to help others?

Empaths often find separating their true identity from the emotions of others quite difficult. One author likened Empaths to idealists. Individuals who are social visionaries that deeply contemplate on ways to help the world around them. The fervent need to analyze others and *"fix"* their emotional issues can turn Empathy into a compulsion. Often, when responding to the words, demeanor, and actions of others, Empaths tend to conclude the very situation at hand. If perceived to be negative, an Empath will do everything they can to fix the issue. Although admirable, this can cause emotional co-dependency. The reliance on others happiness to feel satisfied.

Many attribute co-dependency as being financially or emotionally reliant on another person to care for them. Although true, co-dependency with Empaths can look a bit different. Instead of relying on the other person to take care of their issues, they do the opposite. They rely heavily on what they can do to make their friend or partner happier to gain personal satisfaction. Placing so much energy into trying to please others is draining. To seek independence, an Empath has to set reasonable limits to what they allow themselves to do.

For example, a highly sensitive woman is in a relationship. One day, her husband comes home from a stressful day at work, with a lackluster attitude. He barely speaks, slams doors, and even locks himself in his room. Being an Empath, the wife automatically picks up on his behavior and now begins to feel a great deal of stress herself. She acts on ways to improve his mood, but nothing works. He continues to come home daily in a rut. The need to make him feel better is at the height of the wife's to-do list. So much so, she neglects her priorities. This is an example of co-dependence. The wife can do all she can to improve the mood of her husband, but if the issue is rooted in his job, *he* has to decide to do something about it. It is not her responsibility. Therefore, she has to gain personal independence from the situation at hand.

Have you encountered a similar situation? Perhaps the emotions of others have clouded your ability to accomplish your tasks. If so, you first need to analyze where the issue is coming from. If it is an outside source such as job or family troubles, all you can do is offer support. You cannot fix something that is out of your control. After you have offered your support, either verbally or physically, let it be. Allow your friend or partner the freedom to overcome their stress. Since you are an energy absorber, limit your association with them until they are balanced. You can still be there for someone and Empathize with their distress without sacrificing your sanity.

Stand Firm in Your Personality

An Empath advocate once quoted, "(on Empaths and their dealings with others) They often practice a kindness that compromises the self."[10] Highly sensitive people understand how conflict can negatively impact their energy. By simply being exposed to an argument or disagreement can cause them a great deal of stress. Therefore,

---

[10] Thor, E. (2018). Personal Growth Influencer. The Hidden Issues of the Empath. Available at: https://www.erikthor.com/2017/01/09/issues-of-the-empath/

Empaths typically avoid any form of conflict, even if it means standing up for their beliefs. Often, this leads them down a path of being taken advantage of.

In general, the term *highly-sensitive person* is a topic rarely discussed. If anything, these individuals are placed in the mentally unstable category. You can take pride in your ability by owning it. Being an Empath is nothing to be ashamed of. In fact, the ability to pick up on the emotions of others and feel intensely is something many crave. When others seem to doubt your condition, stand up for yourself! Do not allow anyone to demean your neurological makeup simply because they cannot understand it. By educating yourself on your personality gift, it will be easier to explain your needs to others.

No doubt you have repressed emotions that stem from situations where you knew you should have spoken up but held back. One way to overcome your fear of standing up for yourself is to change your personal definition of conflict. Disagreements are a natural part of life being that we are all drastically different. Instead of viewing conflict as being something overwhelmingly negative, it's wise to view it as a natural part of life. There is nothing taboo about standing up for something you believe in. In fact, speaking up may be a way to gain respect. In a calm and collected manner, speak your mind with confidence. Don't succumb to displaying anger, irritation, or even fear. Rather, view your advocacy is mere words with power, words that are no different from a casual conversation. By doing so, you won't feel the fear or pressure associated with speaking up. Instead, you will be firm in your dealings.

Advocate for Your Needs

As mentioned, Empaths are extremely compassionate individuals with a longing to make others happy. Often, others feel extremely comfortable with confiding in an Empath during stressful times. Do you find yourself constantly having to listen to the problems of others? Do these transactions leave you drained and unable to focus on what you are doing? Do you sometimes fear to reach out to a trusted confidant for help when you need it?

Being your own self-advocate will work wonders for your energy field. Freely express your needs, even if it is initially uncomfortable. In the event that it does inconvenience someone else, allow it for your own needs. Your health is far more important than the preconceived notions of others. This is not a selfish mentality, but a necessary one if you want to contain your balance. The people you choose to associate with should deeply care about your health needs. Express to them what an Empath is. It's likely; they have probably never been exposed to highly sensitive individuals. Let them know your triggers, and specific situation or entertainment you dislike. In addition, explain that your personal time is absolutely necessary. By speaking up for yourself, you will likely gain the support of those around you.

Empaths have such a strong innate desire to help others that they may feel uncomfortable venting to friends and family members. Do you find it increasingly difficult to confide in a loved one when you feel overwhelmed? Do you even experience guilt when expressing these emotions? If so, you likely avoid verbally expressing yourself. In turn, you repress emotions that desperately need an outlet. You have to understand that you are a valuable and important member of this world. Your thoughts and feelings matter just as much as the next. It is nothing wrong with needing a shoulder to lean on at times. A conversation with a listening ear may help to recharge your energy.

You are a unique individual with a unique set of goals, and aspirations. Perhaps others may not fully understand your interests. This may prompt them to project their opinions on yours. When making decisions, others may not fully understand your intuitive abilities. You may encounter others trying to make important decisions for you as opposed to letting you create your path. An Empath, you have an instinctual gift that allows you to feel what's right. Listen to that voice and proceed, when others attempt to make you feel bad for your goals, continue on your path. Let them know you are deeply rooted in your decisions. By doing so, you will develop a higher level of self-respect and others will feed off of that.

Become Transparent with Your Expectations of Others

As an Empath, you feel deeply. You can easily read the reactions of others, and that can lead to overthinking. Have you ever carried on a conversation with someone else, only to go home and analyze every minute detail? This compulsive behavior could lead to concluding how the person feels about you. Also, you may feel disappointed when others don't show the same level of compassion or Empathy as you would. This is when practicing a realistic mentality comes into play.

Chapter 4: Keeping Your Sanity-How to Reach Satisfaction in Your Relationships

In a perfect world, everyone would show immense levels of kindness and understanding for others. The reality is, there are evil and narcissistic people walking this earth without a care for others. As an Empath, you have to understand that not everyone feels the way you do. Not everyone has the emotional capacity to take on the emotions and burdens of others. Although a foreign concept to you, that's the reality for some. You cannot change the way each person thinks. What you can change, is your perspective. You can choose to understand that not everyone is as compassionate to help others as you are. By doing so, you won't be disappointed by the actions of others. Rather, you will understand their perspective and move on.

Other people are also going to make decisions that directly conflict with your own. Despite your best intentions, they may go left while you encouraged right. If that occurs, *let it be*. Everyone has their responsibility to make adequate decisions for their future. As an Empath, you may harp on the consequences of others actions. Do not allow that energy to permeate your vibration. Instead, acknowledge that they made an opposing choice and moved forward. The only expectations you should rely on are those you set for yourself. This will save you a lot of time and energy in the future.

It is quite possible to avoid being a giving machine when dealing with others. If you constantly give of yourself, embody the emotions of others, and repress your own needs, crazy would be an understatement! As previously highlighted, you deserve the world. Your attraction to kindness is a revered quality that should be praised. You can obtain satisfaction within your relationships while living as a highly sensitive person. But, satisfaction requires more than owning your gift.

As an Empath, setting limits and boundaries when dealing with others is vital. In the next chapter, we'll dive into situational occurrences that frequently happen to Empaths. After reading these tips, you will have the confidence to set the proper boundaries and preserve your energy.

Chapter 5:
Protect Your Energy - Key Tips for Remaining Balanced and Setting Limits

L imit setting is crucial to maintaining your sanity as a highly sensitive person. The amount of over-stimulating elements you encounter daily is draining. Highly sensitive people are not only vulnerable to the emotional dumping of others. They are also quite sensitive to loud noises, bright lights, and even harsh climates. Also, Empaths can drastically alter in mood; beginning the day feeling happy only to feel withdrawn soon after. The importance of protecting your energy in this regard is imperative. You cannot control the elements you may encounter, but you can prepare for them. However, you may come to a point when you have reached your emotional limit. When this occurs, how can you set proper limits and create healthy boundaries?

Take a Time Out

When working, going out, or even hosting an event, it's important to know when you need a break. At this point, your loved ones are probably well aware of your needs, and they respect them. The issue may present itself in the professional environment. Colleagues, bosses, and supervisors often lack Empathy. They are focused on getting the job done quickly and efficiently.

This means you have a unique opportunity to hone in on your limit setting skills. For example, when you receive an e-mail, do you jump at the opportunity to answer it? Even if it means sacrificing your morning coffee, or handling another task? If so, you aren't setting the proper boundaries, and you will continue to be taken advantage of. Author and fellow highly sensitive person Carolina Van Kimmenade shares her experience with being an Empath in the workplace. She explains, "For a while, I made the mistake of responding to people instantly and making time for unexpected meetings. I thought I was just service-oriented...The result? I was giving off the message that I had oodles of time, and hence, few people respected my time. So, I started weeding out the essential from the non-essential e-mails by NOT responding immediately. I responded to e-mail once a day and started claiming my lunch hour no matter what."[11]

When this occurs, acknowledge the e-mail and continue to take care of your needs first. As a highly sensitive person, your first inclination is to help even if that means sacrificing your well-being. Being called on at a whim to perform tasks or duties for others is inconsiderate and an ultimate sign of disrespect. If someone does not respect your time or availability, they don't respect you as a person. Remember, you cannot

---

[11] Van Kimmenade, C. (2011). The Happy Sensitive. Essential Boundaries for HSPs and Empaths. Available at:
https://thehappysensitive.com/essential-boundaries-for-hsps-and-empaths-keeping-track-of-our-own-well-being/

pour from an empty pot. Ensure that your pot is full of taking on anything additional. You will find that you can perform at a higher level when you feel good!

We previously discussed taking a timeout during big events. Bathrooms, cars, and even stepping outside can be a great retreat. But, what if that simply isn't possible. A new mother may find leaving her crying baby so she can take a time out quite difficult. This is where mindful breathing and relaxation strategies count. If you are in a situation where you are emotionally drained, stop. Approach this situation, in the same manner; you would an anxiety or panic attack. Begin to focus on your senses. Calmly fixate on something near you, and begin to breathe. You will notice that despite the chaos around you, you are centered and relaxed. This mini break can be likened to a healthy snack that holds you over until dinner time.

Keep Your Empath Tool Kit with You

As mentioned, there are many tools useful for Empaths and highly sensitive people to utilize throughout the day. If you suffer from light, sound, or temperature sensitivities, it is important to be prepared for whatever the day could bring. One way to protect your energy is to invest in noise canceling headphones. The beauty in these is that they now come in travel sized options. The previous bulky headphones are now able to fit discreetly in your ear.

Make good use of these when dealing with a noisy car or train rides, or a hectic work environment. Also, bring small scarf's or sweaters with you when the environment changes. You may find that being in a too humid or cold environment could cause distress. When you are prepared, you can protect your energy and have more control over your balance. Some even like to bring essential oils with them as a refresher throughout the day. Some oils are so small; they can fit in the palm of your hand!

Understand the Energy Vampires and Avoid Them

A popular phrase amongst the Empath and highly sensitive community are emotional, energy vampires. These individuals are those who drain you of your energy either through their drama-filled lives, or their negative energy. If you realize that you may have a few characteristics of a highly sensitive person, likely, you were going off of a certain feeling after finishing an exchange with someone else. Perhaps it was a feeling of guilt, confusion, fatigue, and even stress. In hindsight, you were associating with an emotional vampire who sucked your positive energy away! Let's consider a few characteristics of the energy vampire.

Empath

- They constantly complain about their current situation. Despite being offered advice, they continue to complain without seeking a solution.

- Gossip, current events, and the mishaps of others are their topic of conversation.

- They constantly attempt to derail you from making your own choices. They may suggest alternative options that they believe are in your best interests.

- They need something from you constantly.

- They are domineering, condescending, and controlling. Often masking themselves as gregarious or helpful.

Energy vampires are not bad people. They simply have not been educated on how to communicate and deal with others properly.

Chapter 5: Protect Your Energy - Key Tips for Remaining Balanced and Setting Limits

They've lived their entire lives accepting from others. Nobody has taken the time to show them what a healthy relationship looks like. They're accustomed to getting their way. As opposed to simply relying on a hunch, look for the characteristics above of the people you choose to associate with. Analyze their topics of conversation, actions, interests, and even body language, to determine if you want to be around them. Once you have identified them, limit, if not completely cut off, your ties with them.

There will be certain situations where communication is unavoidable. When that occurs, deflection is key. As an Empath, you can sense when the conversation begins to spiral into negativity. Simply ignore the comment or change the subject. If possible, limit your interaction with that person so you can enjoy the remainder of your time without feeling drained. Remember, you are in control of your energy.

Detox from Technology

Technology is a caveat of bittersweet uses. It allows highly sensitive people the opportunity to communicate virtually, but it can also trigger energy vampires into thinking you are always available. Also, social media has become a breeding ground for heartbreaking news articles and negativity. Sometimes, social media can be the energy lurking vampire in disguise. Do you ever feel drained after scrolling through your Facebook or Instagram feed? Could you be taking in the negative energy of others even through excessive screen time?

Social media and technology cleanse have been known to restore energy levels and promote mental clarity. Limit yourself to only 30 minutes a day of social media and technology. Children who deal with neurological imbalances are cautioned against excessive screen time use. Instead, they are encouraged to participate in outside activities that stimulate certain functions of the brain. By doing so, their hemispheres become balanced which encourages advanced cognitive thinking. If setting technology boundaries is effective for children who have dyslexia or ADHD, surely it is beneficial for the entire population.

Set Social Limits

Maintaining a healthy social life is something many counselors of highly sensitive people encourage. This promotes good social skills and is a great form of recreation since many Empathic people are prone to seclusion. However, you need to set adequate limits for yourself when it comes to attending social events. Your hope for mental clarity should outweigh your feelings of obligation to the event. Perhaps you should allow yourself two events per month. When it comes to outings with friends, set a time limit as well as an "*out*" phrase.

This can be used when you are drained and desperately need to leave. Perhaps leave a low priority task undone so you can use that as a reason to leave. One Empath always plans before scheduling time with friends. "I always set aside one class or task a day as an 'emergency fund' for when I am exhausted from being around others. I simply say, 'I need to take care of so and so,' and I'm gone. I feel more in control over my social schedule, and my friends understand." As you become savvy with centering exercises, you can increase this amount as you begin to progress.

Energy perseverance and protection is essential to have a healthy interaction with others. Setting proper boundaries and limits to your social schedule will prevent you from becoming overly drained by the emotions of others. Being a recluse is counterproductive to your energy. Little social interaction can uplift you in times of distress. Setting social limits should be taken seriously as these occasions can be mentally draining.

Securing your energy is essential to living as a highly sensitive person. Not only is your ability to handle stimulating situations emotionally different from others, but it is also biologically unique. Your energy field is valuable and something to be protected. This serves as protection against energy consuming situations that impact productivity. Now that we have the reasoning behind securing your energy with an emphasis on its importance let's consider a few interactive exercises that will help you to restore your energy and nurture your sensitivities.

Chapter 6:
Integrative Techniques to Restore Energy and Nurture Sensitivities

Integrative therapy has gained popularity over the years by combining many forms of positive coping strategies in an attempt to reach wellness. Previously, medication and counseling were the primary options that those seeking help were given. Now, animals, nature, the arts, and holistic options are incorporated in the healing process. However, being highly sensitive is not a matter of mental health care. Empaths and highly sensitive individuals may experience symptoms of depression, anxiety, and even bipolar disorder as a result of being consistently overwhelmed. When your energy is being compromised or even drained, certain integrative techniques can be applied to restoring balance. Let's consider a few practical techniques that could assist with self-exploration and balance.

Palliative Care

Patients who are cancer survivors or even individuals who are terminally ill, partake in activities called palliative arts. According to

CURE, the hub for cancer research, they define palliative arts as, "the belief that engaging in purposeful activity can enrich and add meaning to life, even during treatment for a serious illness."[12] This means of therapy prompts patients to face their emotions through poetry, painting, sculpting, and music. This allows participants to focus primarily on their negative emotions in conjunction with their debilitating illness and express that positively. Many Empaths find great solace in expressing their thoughts through poetry. In fact, a popular website entitled Warrior Poet Wisdom shares beautiful poetry written by highly sensitive people from around the world.

---

[12] Leonard, L. (2017). CURE. Cancer Updates, Research & Education. The Healing Arts in Palliative Care. Available at: https://www.curetoday.com/publications/cure/2017/fall-2017/the-healing-arts-in-palliative-care

Empaths

There is a type of person who

Is known as an Empath

While many think that they are blessed

They don't know of the wrath

That comes with being so in tune

With other people's feelings

That for the Empath, even the

Most casual of dealings

Can uncover strong feelings of

Much fear, hate or mistrust

The Empath can pick up on things

Even if not discussed

A super-human attention

To detail that reveals

How a smiling, joking person

Actually feels

Some pick up an energy

Chapter 6: Integrative Techniques to Restore Energy and Nurture Sensitivities

While others just go by

Body language, chosen words

Or the look in their eye

The Empath is a sensitive

Compassionate observer

Many times they lose themselves

Amid another's fervor

Shackled with acuity

They often lose control

Of their own thoughts and feelings cause

Another does cajole

They're overwhelmed by the influence

Of what rages around

Every detail magnified

And amplified each sound

Lucky or a blessing? No,

Most Empaths feel they're cursed

Because each day they are a witness

Empath

To humanity's worst
The selfishness, the fear, the lack
Of any hope
The whining and complaining and
The masses who mope
The Empath knows there's strength inside
Themselves and everyone
They're cursed to watch most people simply
Ignore it and shun
The Empath sees the beauty in
The little things each day
But also sees the countless people
That piss it away
The Empath is a noble guard
A listener to all
They are the ones that you just can't
Help but tear down your wall
And open up to, speak to, be

Chapter 6: Integrative Techniques to Restore Energy and Nurture Sensitivities

Vulnerable, exposed

Because the Empath's mind is never

Ignorant and closed

They are the listeners who care

Who truly hear your tale?

Who do relate to what you're going

Through each time you fail

And they sustain a lot of wear

And tear from what they do

If only all knew what it's like

To have an Empathic view

To let go of yourself and walk

A mile in their shoes

To feel their pain and not be able

To even refuse

Here's to Empaths, blessed and cursed

With great acuity

True Warrior Poets who

Empath

Just wish they could be free

But that is not their lot in life

No, that is not their mission

In a world of ignorance

Their purpose is cognition

To listen, understand and teach

People about themselves

To be the fearless explorer

Who boldly deeper delves?

Keep in mind what energy

You do choose to put out

You never know when an Empath

Maybe lurking about.[13]

---

[13] Miro (2013). Warrior Poets Wisdom. Empath. Available at: https://warriorpoetwisdom.com/2012/07/25/empaths/

Chapter 6: Integrative Techniques to Restore Energy and Nurture Sensitivities

The sentiments expressed in the featured poem is how many bring to life their repressed emotions. Empaths and highly sensitive people generally shy away from expressing their inner demons to others. Art with a purpose allows them the opportunity to release those emotions without the fear of judgment.

Acupuncture Treatment

Highly sensitive people tend to carry stress in their belly and lower backs. Acupuncture treatment utilizes small needles to regulate energy being blocked by various ailments. Ancient Chinese practitioners refer to a person's balance or energy regulation as their "*chi.*" By carefully placing the small needles at specific points around the body, this form of treatment has multiple uses. Some include anxiety, fatigue, body pain, and even depression. Since it focuses so much on energy regulation, it is ideal for a highly sensitive person who wants to regain their sense of balance.

Re-wire Your Habitual Thinking

Dr. Joseph Cardillo, PH.D. Writes about the importance of recreating our behavioral templates. These templates are patterns of thinking that soon turn into excuses. They block growth and impede on personal development. When feeling overly stimulated by a person or a chaotic situation, it can be easy to let the time pass without taking action simply. Your mind is so accustomed to helping others; you use your compassion as a crutch.

By rewiring the way you approach certain situations, you will see a dramatic change in your tolerance level. You will no longer allow others to dump their emotions on you, nor will you remain a victim. Instead, you can recognize self-destructive behavioral patterns and adjust them.

Re-wiring your thinking takes time and a great deal of patience. For Empaths, self-perfection is a constant struggle.

In order to properly reach your goals, you have to give yourself the opportunity to fail. This way, you can learn how to restore your energy when defeated. Benjamin Franklin said it best, "energy and persistence conquer all things." If your energy is deflated, how can you expect to make the necessary changes? Take action every day to build your confidence and act on your intuition.

Define Your Mantra

Empaths and highly sensitive people have the unique gift of being able to read others. However, their ability to distinguish their inward emotions is often confusing. Mantras are short, expressive sentences that are the guideposts for your everyday life. They are more than just motivational quotes. They are affirmations that speak peace into existence. Many find it crucial to repeat certain phrases before engaging in social activities or spending time with others. The wonderful thing about mantras is that you have the power to choose your words. Some popular phrases include:

1. I am strong, and I will protect myself from the energy of others.

2. I will speak up for myself and express my needs.

3. I will remove myself from toxic situations without being ashamed.

Make these sayings your daily reminder that you can conquer the world without feeling intimidated. Doing so will help to keep you centered and grounded before leaving the house.

Breema Bodywork

Breema is an alternative form of massage therapy that centers the body and mind. A typical session involves the client being placed in specific stretches facilitated by the therapist. Many of the stretches focus on the entire body and can look similar to traditional yoga moves. The stretches are designed to help regulate energy flow while promoting mental stability. During the session, the therapist will gently touch different areas of the body. The beauty behind Breema is that it allows the client to restore their energy through focusing on the present while allowing the therapist to gently massage body, relieving negative stressors.

How to Nurture Your Sensitivities

Mothers are known for nurturing their children to boost development. In fact, research studies have shown that children who were nurtured from birth can cope with stressful situations and retain information well into adulthood.[14] The concept of nurturing means instilling confidence in the person or object in order to promote growth. Through loving actions and positive reinforcement, a weak person or plant can regain strength.

Living with high sensitivities, it is easy to feel defeated when emotions seem to be overwhelming personally. In fact, society looks down upon individuals who outwardly express their emotions. Despite the negative connotations, there is a great strength insensitivity. To find that inner warrior, you have to nurture your sensitivities much like you would a child or a plant.

---

[14] Castro, J. (2012). Live Science. How A Mother's Love Changes A Child's Brain. Available at: https://www.livescience.com/18196-maternal-support-child-brain.html

Reward Your Sensitivities

Being aware of the emotions of others is a gift. When facing situations where you can help a friend, reward yourself with kind words. When you can give in a healthy manner, do something nice for yourself as well. This creates a balance that tells your body that you matter. You are still able to care for others the way you are naturally inclined to and celebrate yourself as well. As an Empath, you are not seeking a reward from others or even acknowledgment. The assistance alone is what gives you gratification. When someone wants to pay you back, so to speak, allow them that opportunity. Do not allow guilt to creep in and defer you from the offer. You deserve to be treated with ultimate kindness as well.

Awareness Promotes Growth

One of the primary ways to nurture sensitivities is to become aware of them. Previously, we discussed how decoding your triggers can help to assist with stress management. Now, it's important that you begin to understand why certain sensitivities affect you so deeply. Could it be a repressed experience that happened during your childhood? Do you have unresolved issues with a particular person that leads you to be deeply impacted by the actions of others?

All of these questions lead to self-discovery that will help to identify the meaning behind your sensitivities. Growth occurs when ignorance fades. Nurture your ability to learn about yourself. This requires you to face past head-on challenges. Sure, it will be an emotional purge that could be difficult, but self-awareness is worth the struggle. Often, licensed professionals who are familiar with highly sensitive individuals can help you on your journey to discovery.

Express Gratitude for Your Body and Soul

When a mother nurtures her child, much of that love comes from gratitude. Motherhood is not guaranteed for all women. Therefore, the experience is sacred, and the mother takes it seriously. She does all she can to provide the best care for her ability in order to secure her child's future. Do you view your body and soul in the same manner?

Showing gratitude for your body involves being mindful of the foods you eat as well as the amount of physical activity you engage in. Express that gratitude through eating nutritious foods and staying away from the harmful elements of this world. Your soul is vast and is complex in its needs. Discover what feeds your soul and makes your spirit rejoice. Anna

Quindlen quoted, "You are the only person alive who has sole custody of your life...your entire life...not just the life your mind, but the life of your heart. Not just your bank account, but your soul."

Every day we are faced with choices. We can choose to succumb to the same crowd of energy draining individuals simply because they're who we are accustomed to. Or, we could choose to do what's best for our soul, and spend time with positive individuals. One highly sensitive woman shared her experience with energy draining vampires during her younger years. She explains, "Once you've been around draining individuals for so long, you begin to grow dependent on their company. The negative conversations become routine, so much so, you don't see the danger of it. You even grow accustomed to the draining feeling. It becomes much harder to find new people to engage with because you are afraid of change."

Although difficult, you have the chance to remove those negative people from your life and start new. Sure, it may be uncomfortable initially, but you will soon reap the benefits of mental clarity. By doing so, you are taking the first steps towards nurturing your soul by providing a safe, and uplifting environment for growing in.

Liken yourself to a beautiful orchid. Orchids thrive in humid, wet environments. What happens if you were to place that plant in the desert, surrounded by sand? When given too much sun, the petals begin to dry out. The leaves would have no moisture to retain. Eventually, the orchid would wither away. However, when put in a tropical climate, the orchid begins to thrive and blossom. It is happy, relaxed, and able to grow. You're the orchid that needs a specific environment to survive. Nurture yourself by changing your draining environment, and creating a space where you can grow.

Also, you have the ability to choose how you view yourself. Living as an Empath or a highly sensitive person is a privilege. Do you view yourself in that manner? You can decide to accept your gift as something unique, or you can attempt to suppress it in an attempt to fit in. The issue with trying to change who you are is that you will constantly have inner turmoil. This inconsistency drains energy and promotes self-loathing. Instead, you could take the necessary steps towards self-acceptance, and be free. This promotes confidence, mental clarity, and preserves energy.

Create a Community

The popularity of highly sensitive people has grown over the last few years. More and more individuals are sharing their stories along with helpful tips. Embrace the culture you belong to and find support for individuals who face the same personality traits. In fact, countless support groups offer a sense of friendship and understanding for Empathic individuals. There, you can learn helpful tips on how to avoid energy vampires and protect your energy effectively. You may even create meaningful relationships through networking with like-minded individuals.

There are countless alternative ways to restore your energy. Despite criticism, it is imperative to seek out integrative means of therapy that work best for you. In addition, nurturing your body and soul is essential to taking control of your life, and accepting what you are given. By doing so, you will view your capabilities as something praiseworthy as opposed to shameful. In the next chapter, we will analyze how to gain control of your life without compromising your politeness.

Chapter 7:
How to Ignore Others-Polite and Effective Ways to Focus on Your Own Emotions

As an Empath, you likely have trouble with standing up for your own emotions. This could be as a result of fear, or, it could stem from wanting to keep the peace. We previously discussed how to handle conflict properly. Now, it's time to decode polite and practical ways to taking back your control and maintaining your space. Many people attribute being polite to meekness. While being meek is a respectable quality, it is only a compliment to politeness.

Empath

The dictionary defines polite, as, "having or showing behavior that is respectful and considerate of other people." Highly sensitive individuals understand the importance of being kind and considerate. In fact, when treated with a lack of kindness, Empaths can be quite offended for some time. There is a difference between being polite and being submissive. As a highly sensitive person, you may feel inclined to submit to the other person's wishes or desires in order to avoid conflict. This may even be confused with being polite.

However, the issue occurs when being polite compromises you of your desires, wishes, and needs. Do you often feel that your politeness has held you back from getting something you wanted? In your dealings with others, do you often allow people to drain you of your energy because you don't want to make them feel bad or uncomfortable? Let's consider how to maintain your energy politely effectively.

When Dealing with Energy Vampires

Narcissists, needy individuals, and energy vampires are all drawn to highly sensitive people because they can sense their nurturing nature. They like being able to dump all of their problems on them because Empaths are amazing listeners. Does this sound familiar? One of the breeding grounds for energy vampires is in the workplace. Deadlines, rude managers, and unfair pay are all reasons for unhappiness. As a highly sensitive person, you are in tune with these injustices anyway. Likely, you have to deal with them on your own.

Since you have a compassionate heart, a co-worker may find comfort with unloading his or her problems on you. This could impact your productivity and even ruin the morale of the office. How can you effectively tell him or her that you can no longer carry their burden? One way is to set boundaries vocally. When you see the energy vampire approaching your desk, politely tell them, "I understand your frustrations, but let's work on practical ways we can improve our work environment. Maybe you can bring them up to our human resources department." This statement acknowledges their pain without dismissing it as unimportant. It also opens to door for them to take action. In other words, dump their troubles on someone else. This is still a polite way of maintaining your space while still helping a co-worker.

This polite way of ignoring the person may initially take some practice. They say it takes three times to solidify a habit. The energy vampire may not even notice your slight curve at first. However, if you continue to shut them down politely, they will eventually get the point.

Chapter 7: How to Ignore Others-Polite and Effective Ways to Focus on Your Own Emotions

If this person continues to annoy you with negativity, it may be wise to take it a step further and be honest with them.

You don't have to say, "You're an energy vampire, and I cannot deal with you anymore." Rather, one polite option is, "I appreciate that you feel comfortable confiding in me. But, I am trying to maintain my peace of mind in this chaotic environment. Maybe we could start talking about positive aspects of our day." This will show the person that you still want to be kind to them, but you would prefer to redirect the conversations to something productive. Often, energy vampires don't even realize the nature of their complaints. By politely letting them know, this may encourage them to do some self-reflection.

These tips can also be applied to interpersonal relationships as well. Fortunately, it is easier to speak openly with friends or family members.

Empath

When faced with energy draining friends, it may be wise to take the blunt approach. Your friend cares about you and likely wants to keep you in their life. However, friendship revolves around more than complaining, venting, and problem dumping. Explain to them that you want to be their friend, but you physically cannot manage all of their problems. Honesty is truly the best policy if you want people to get the point truly. You are constantly taking on the emotions of others, and that isn't fair. You deserve to have a great quality of life. This can only occur when you verbally set these boundaries.

It's Okay to Be Transparent

Many people were raised to believe that being honest about your feelings, equates to being rude. There is a blurred shade of grey that separates honesty and rudeness. That area is called tone. The way you say something can turn a transparent, stream of expression, into an

offensive argument. Is there a way to be honest
with your friends and romantic partners without
coming off as rude?

When Empaths are dating, some may find that
constant togetherness can be a cause of distress
and anxiety. It isn't because they dislike the
person, they just need time to recharge. When
facing the challenge of setting limits and
boundaries in a romantic relationship, open
communication is key. It is wise to explain your
disposition to others, so they don't misinterpret
your actions. Some useful phrases include:

- I really enjoy your company, but sometimes
  I need some time to myself. It's not that I
  don't like you, I just become overwhelmed
  easily and need to recharge.

- I highly value my quiet, alone time. I hope
  you can understand and respect this.

Empath

By letting them know that you do enjoy their company, it eliminates confusion with regards to your feelings. Your partner won't think they are doing something wrong. Rather, they will understand that this is a part of who you are.

The topic of telling someone you are highly sensitive is subjective to each person. If you feel that you have reached a certain level of comfort with a person, by all means, share your gift with them. By printing articles, researching information, and providing legitimate resources for them, they may better understand your disposition. One husband shared his experience with confessing his sexual addiction to his wife. "While the conversation was initially uncomfortable, I realized that explaining my biological makeup openly and honestly; she was able to understand my condition. We are now able to develop together, positive coping strategies. Without my telling her, she would have been left in the dark with regards to an extremely important aspect of my personality."

While being a highly sensitive person is different from an addiction, the point is still applicable. Being an Empath is a part of who you are. It doesn't define you, but it impacts certain behaviors and decisions. By sharing this with a trusted loved one, you may feel energized. If they are truly there for you, they will listen to your expressions and do their best to seek understanding.

Master the Art of Ignoring

Sometimes ignoring negative sources of energy is essential. After making polite attempts at expressing your needs, some, unfortunately, will not take the hint. This is where ignoring negative energy comes into play. The dictionary defines *ignore*, as, "refuse to take notice of or acknowledge; disregard intentionally." Although harsh, drastic measures must sometimes be taken to protect your energy. When you cannot help but absorb the energy of those around you, your control is imperative. Ignoring someone's negative energy isn't rude. In fact, it is simply a part of life. It is something you need to cultivate in order to survive as an Empath. When you disregard or refuse to take notice of someone else's negativity, you are not putting the person down. Rather, you are choosing to protect your energy without giving into their devices. This may mean setting limits to the association, logging off the computer, or even changing seats in order to achieve that peace. It is not a dismissive quality, but rather, an essential one. A few ways to achieve this are:

1. Create distance between you and the person.

2. Don't engage in their negativity. Respond to their negativity with positivity.

3. If in extreme cases, delete them from social media, and block their number from your phone.

Know When to Walk Away

It is never easy to end a relationship or friendship with someone who has been a part of your life. However, if someone else simply doesn't understand your needs, they aren't worth keeping around. They will only continue to drain you of your energy and soak up your time. There is power in eliminating people from your life. This involves cutting all ties whether electronically or in person.

One key way of knowing when it is time to cut ties is when your emotional levels have reached their peak. Intuitively, you may have an uneasy feeling when a specific person comes around. Listen to that feeling. Your body is trying to communicate something to you, and it requires action. Often, when cutting people off, this doesn't involve a lengthy discussion.

Perhaps slowly backing away is all that is needed. Limit your conversations and don't respond as consistently. However, if your friend or partner wants to know your reasons for needing space, let them know. Explain to them that you are refusing to tolerate their energy and negativity. Explain how it affects your mood and health. This can be done by explaining how their actions have impacted your ability to function and how the drama is draining you. When seeking optimal peace, you have to become comfortable with letting other people know your needs. Even if it means being blatantly honest. You are taking control of the kind of people you want in your life which in turn gives you control over your energy. You will then have more time to focus on your needs, what you want, and how to live a purposeful life.

Chapter 7: How to Ignore Others-Polite and Effective Ways to Focus on Your Own Emotions

Identify Your Tribe

As a highly sensitive person, it is important to create a support system of strong individuals who have your best interests at heart. These can be called, your *tribe*. Ancient civilizations relied heavily on the entire community in order for it to survive. Everyone knew their place and sought out to complete their job to the best of their ability. A social circle can be likened to a tribe. In order for everyone to thrive, there has to be some level of responsibility placed upon each member. Each person has the job to provide support and unconditional love for their friend.

When you choose your tribe, make a list of individuals who support your goals, don't drain your energy, and inspire you. People who go beyond the basic expectations such as loyalty and trust are ideal. These are the ones who understand when you need your space, and they don't become overtly offended. Find these people and invest your time and energy with them. Being an Empath doesn't equate to a life of seclusion. You can have meaningful and purposeful relationships with the right individuals who respect you.

Separating yourself from draining individuals don't have to be a drawn-out process of drama. Rather, you can get your point across in a diligent way without making the other person, or yourself, uncomfortable. All it takes is an effective practice. Sure, initially you may feel anxious.

Imagine this, would you rather continue engaging with this person, only to compromise your mental clarity? Or, would you rather *nip the problem in the bud*, and move on to a more balanced life? After multiple occasions where honesty is needed, you will see the beauty in taking control over your energy. There are uplifting individuals out there who are full of positive and inspirational qualities. Seek those individuals and hold tight to them.

Chapter 8:
Self-Care 101 for Empaths

Throughout this e-book, we've discussed the importance of self-care for Empathic and highly sensitive individuals. Quiet, alone, and relaxing moments can be likened to recharging a dying battery. They offer refreshment and peace in a chaotic world.

Make Your Home a Sanctuary

Home should be a place of retreat when the world becomes overwhelming. It should not be a cause for unnecessary stress or drain. One practical way to obtain balance within the home is to remove all forms of clutter. Take some time to throw away old clothes and unnecessary objects that cloud out energy pathways. By doing so, your home will essentially be able to breathe. You'll find comfort in your space without unnecessary feelings of anxiety. Many Empaths have a sensitivity to harsh lighting. Dim lighting, either through candles or salt lamps, can help to create a calming spirit. Since highly sensitive people are lovers of nature, keeping energy regulating plants in the home can help to assist with relaxation. Some include:

1. Peace Lily. This vibrant plant works as an air purifier which removes toxins in the home. Its delicate and unique flowers are also a beautiful complement to any home.

2. Rosemary is a delicate plant that smells comforting and is used to assist with anxiety and sleep patterns.

3. Ivy plants are strong and luxurious. Working as air filters, an ivy plant will

help to eliminate negativity and toxins in the air.

Even if you need to dedicate a specific space to your interests, utilize what you can! Post inspirational quotes around and even incorporate candles or incense into your environment. Make your area a place of refuge.

Do Something Creative Outside

You are naturally drawn to the arts and nature. So why not combine them by doing something creative outside! Many highly sensitive people find a painting or sketching outside relaxing. This gives them an opportunity to unwind and decompress from the world. They can focus primarily on their project without feeling distressed.

Nature can prove to be a real source of inspiration for Empaths seeking to become centered with the earth. Listen to the sound of the trees and express those vibrations through poetry. Smell the allure of the grass beneath you and begin to create that fresh feeling. The wind can calm your soul with an effortless refreshment. Allow yourself the creative freedom to allow nature to take you wherever it wants. As a highly sensitive person, you are accustomed to feeling the feelings of everyone else. By giving your control to the forces around you, you are allowing nature to guide your actions. This slight release is comforting in such a chaotic atmosphere.

Take Time to Remain Still

Relaxing in silence is important for highly sensitive people because it gives them the opportunity to become one with their thoughts in a quiet environment. There are many opportunities to learn when doing nothing. One author quoted, "While most of us find it hard to tolerate in many instances boredom can be a prelude to something. It can trigger our imagination and creativity." Schedule a few minutes each day to allow yourself the opportunity to be bored.

Much like meditation, focus on allowing your thoughts to stream without attempting to control them. This gives your body and your mind some much-needed rest. Often, highly sensitive people may feel that doing nothing equates to lacking productivity. This may even hinge on the perfection complex many Empaths possess. They may feel that they must engage in some activity in order to not be perceived as lazy. This thinking is counterproductive as it essentially forces your mind and body to become overworked. Think of remaining still as conscious sleeping. During sleep, the body has time to rest and release energy. In like manner, remaining still can similarly reenergize your innovation.

Indulge in Relaxation Treatments

There are countless opportunities to engage in doing it yourself relaxation techniques in the comfort of your own home. Many find comfort with ending their night with a cup of tea. Tea, like essential oils, can release relaxing components into the body. Ginger, lavender, and chamomile are all examples of tests that promote wellness. If you've experienced an overstimulating day, why not indulge in a cup of tea when you come home. Many also find the process of tea making quite spiritual in nature.

Also, pampering yourself through beauty treatments is an awesome way to show appreciation for your body while staying frugal. Many food ingredients located within the home have multiple uses for the body. You can create an invigorating body scrub through mixing coffee grounds and coconut oil. Honey is filled with antioxidant properties that can rejuvenate the skin while reducing acne scars. Turmeric, the "golden goddess" of India, is an amazing herb that gives the skin a natural glow. When you take the time to reenergize yourself through pampering, you are showing gratitude for your body. You will be able to decompress without being around people.

Self-care is essential for a highly sensitive person. You can become so drained from giving of yourself and extending your emotions that you forget that you deserve some TLC as well. The purpose of engaging in self-care is to give your mind the opportunity to relax while expressing gratitude and appreciation for your body. This doesn't have to be a daily event. Rather, set aside one hour a week that is dedicated solely to your benefit.

Soon, you will see the difference in how you manage stress. If your time is limited, why not make your daily or nightly routine a sacred experience. By carrying out daily tasks such as brushing your teeth or taking a shower, you can create opportunities for a mini-escape. Play relaxing or uplifting music while preparing yourself for the day. Maybe even utilize this time to repeat your daily mantra. By doing so, you are able to enter the day with confidence in your ability to ward off negativity.

Chapter 9:

How to Conquer Perfectionism

Perfectionism is a harmful obsession that plagues many individuals. It impacts interaction, decision making, and overall mental clarity. The urge to be perfect in an imperfect world can be likened to attempting to count the stars. It's simply impossible. The will to be perfect is centered on a deeply rooted expectation that was placed upon individuals from an early age. This could be a parent expecting their child to bring home all A's or a spouse seeking a spotless home. Often, these experiences are not met with positive reinforcement. Rather, when the individuals at hand did not meet the expectations set, they were likely given negative feedback which impacted their confidence.

This manner of child-rearing is extremely detrimental to highly sensitive children. In fact, one highly sensitive child constantly asks, "why do my parents hate me?" He felt an intense self-loathing because he couldn't meet the high expectations of his parents. Imagine living a life out of your means. It would likely result in repressed emotions, resentment, and possibly depression. Did you ever feel like that highly sensitive child?

Living as an Empath, you have likely encountered individuals who have expectations of your behavior. They expect you to always listen to them, abide by their values, and subscribe to their way of thinking. Previously, we touched on how to overcome those expectations and learn to lean on your own intuition. However, there is a flip-side to perfectionism that doesn't involve negative criticism from an outside source. Highly sensitive people have impeccable perception. They are able to see when something isn't right and even feel when conflict is rising.

This gift comes with a caveat of expecting perfection from yourself and others. Let's illustrate. A highly sensitive person is listening in on a conversation between two co-workers in the workplace. The first is expressing how his mother is terminally ill and is not expected to survive. Obviously upset, he begins to explain his stressors. The second co-worker, in a dry and unenthusiastic tone, says, "Well, maybe you should try to push it out of your mind. We are all going through something." The highly sensitive person listening immediately cringes at the lack of Empathy displayed. This causes her to become angry at the uninterested co-worker. She cannot understand how someone could not feel the pain of another. In an attempt to control the feelings of others, she is immediately plagued by the rush of emotions. Could this be a sign of expected perfectionism?

Highly sensitive people may project their expectations of how others should behave which blocks their ability to make purposeful relationships. Also, they may become increasingly down on themselves when situations don't work out. For example, pickles may be the snack of choice for some, while others cringe at the sight of the green cucumber. There is nothing wrong with either opinion. However, the similarity is perception. What works for some may not work for everyone else. An Empath may expect everyone around them to think the way they do and even behave in the same manner. This creates frustration and a disappointment. Have you noticed that your recent feelings of mistrust and even distress could be guided by expecting too much from others? If so, you are not alone in your feelings. Let's consider a few ways to balancing perfectionism and learning acceptance.

Accept Things As They Are

Let's face it; things could always be executed better. There is always the looming threat of leveling up with everything. The problem with perfectionism is that there is always going to be something better than the current. That's a part of life. You could climb the highest mountain, but there's always the comparison of an astronaut on making it to the moon. The sooner you begin to accept that there will always be something better, you won't feel the need to search for it constantly. This is especially helpful when setting realistic expectations for yourself.

As an Empath, you may want to take on every problem there is in an attempt to change the world. As admirable as that is, it's impossible. You cannot change every perception, action, or even situation in the world. If you could, the task would have been accomplished. Therefore, learn to accept that there will be a few loose ends. There will be some individuals who choose to go a different route than you think they should. Some people may not show as much Empathy or kindness towards others as you expected them to. That's okay. Trying to reach an impossible peak will only tire your energy and leave you drained. When you feel that you are taking on too many emotions, use that time to stop and breathe. Put down your current task and remove yourself from the toxic environment. Practice your breathing or self-care exercises. This will help to lessen that pressure and increase realistic thinking.

Rely on Yourself and Not the Merits of Others

Perfectionism arises when a person places too much emphasis on the expectations of others on their behavior. They believe that by acting in a certain way and appealing to others, they'll get their instinctual needs met. This is a tricky combination of control, low self-esteem, and manipulation. Although highly sensitive people are not intuitively manipulative, sometimes repressed emotions could come across as co-dependent or heavily rely on others as a source of happiness. When you begin to notice that uncomfortable feeling of giving into what someone else wants of you, emphasis that feeling until you are uncomfortable. Do not ignore it, or pass it off as something normal. Instead, tell yourself that you need to take action to rid yourself of that emotion.

Begin to make small changes in your life that benefit you, without thinking about how someone else may feel. Don't try to make a complete personality change as that may discourage you. Rather, start with simply expressing your needs as opposed to trying to please someone else. Then, move up a step and begin to set limits. Soon, you will be able to rely on yourself instead of living up to the unrealistic expectations set by others. This will impact your decision making as well. You will no longer need the approval of others to make a reliable decision. In turn, you will rely on your own intuition and become free.

Be Easy on Yourself and Others

As an Empath, you have a keen sense of picking up on the vibes of other people. When you meet someone, you instinctively know not to trust that person. You may feel their tone, body movements, or even disposition that leads you to the personal conclusion. Although this may seem helpful in determining who to associate with and who to avoid, this could lead to expecting perfect behavior from everyone around you. Sure, there are narcissistic and uncaring people who are out to drain you of your energy. But, are any of us in a position to judge? Simply because you hold this incredible gift, does that give you the right to deem others as *bad*? Also, can you truly expect others to succumb to behavior that is acceptable to you only?

Learn to be easy on the mishaps of others. There is a clear line between understanding, forgiving, and being taken advantage of. You can easily seek to understand why someone behaves the way they do in order to seek forgiveness. However, forgiving someone does not give them the opportunity to continue taking advantage of your kindness. After forgiveness set those boundaries to keep your energy fluid. Don't compromise your standards in order to appease someone else. Rather, be balanced in your viewing of others and seek understanding.

This can also be applied to how you view social injustices. You feel the sadness, and pain associated with high profile news stories. Does this cause you to go into emotional distress due to the implications of others? If so, these feelings may impact your daily routine or ability to remain balanced. The problem with seeking this level of perfectionism is that it is attempting to control a matter that is beyond your means. Sure, you can feel a sense of Empathy towards a given situation. However, you do not have the power to change it. Many highly sensitive people find positive ways to express this need for change through personal advocacy projects. By making a difference through participating in social changes, you can do your part without feeling overwhelmed. Volunteer with a local organization and find out how you can give back on a smaller scale. This will satisfy your need without compromising your energy.

Highly sensitive Empath and author quoted, "I've been 'suffering' with perfectionism all of my life. I was a perfectionist as a child, and if I made a mistake, I'd feel humiliated and hate myself for it.

Empath

This unhealthy attitude made me an underachiever throughout my school years."[15] Empaths feel the emotions of others on a heightened level. However, as you well know, are increasingly hard on themselves. Allow yourself the opportunity to make mistakes and fail. Through failure, inspiration flows. Without allowing yourself the comfort to fail, you will always maintain a high level of stress that drains your energy.

When you understand that everyone makes mistakes, this will help to relieve that tension. Some find comfort in sharing their feelings through creative outlets. Expressing those emotional needs could be beneficial to their mental well-being.

[15] Harwin, C. (2013). Highly Sensitive Thoughts: I'm Proud to be a perfectionist! Available at: http://highlysensitivethoughts.com/2013/06/10/uncategoized/highly-sensitive-people-im-proud-to-be-a-perfectionist/

Chapter 9: How to Conquer Perfectionism

Perfectionism does not have to be crippling. In fact, seeking unrealistic expectations for yourself and others will only lead to a life of lacking fulfillment. Seek your purpose, but remember to enjoy life in the meantime. Practicing mindfulness will assist you with redeveloping your mind and pushing it towards growth.

Chapter 10:
Embracing Your Gift and How to Find Inner Strength

There is a great deal of strength in being a highly sensitive person. In a world so full of evil and a lack of Empathy, it is refreshing to encounter individuals who feel a lot of what others feel. Individuals who can read the emotions of those they meet without actually engaging in a deep conversation. Having an appreciation for nature in a world that disregards the feelings of the earth is rare. Although debilitating at times, you are resilient in your path. You are a warrior that can defeat negativity. Can you simply become a warrior overnight? No. You have to train to develop that inner strength further. Let's review how to boost that inner strength and reach a level of balance.

You Can Help Others

Being aware of the emotions of others gives you a rare advantage to change lives. As mentioned, many highly sensitive individuals make for excellent doctors, nurses, and psychologists. Being an Empath does not mean you are doomed to a life of seclusion. Instead, you can use your gift and help those around you. You can understand their plights, sadness, and emotions on a personal level. This makes you an ideal listener or even an inspiration to others. Once you've reached a point where you know your limits, you have a developed routine of self-care, and you understand your emotions, you can use those for the betterment of others. Seek to assist those when they confide in you with reasonable advice.

Chapter 10: Embracing Your Gift and How to Find Inner Strength

Also, there are countless numbers of highly sensitive people who are seeking the truth about their characteristics. Some may not fully understand why certain people or situations affect them differently. They could be stuck in a confusing mentality that leads them to be hard on themselves. Since you understand your gift, you are now able to help others fully understand theirs. Use your voice as an advocate for the Empath community. You can help them set reasonable boundaries, limits, and expectations of the world through firsthand experience. By doing so, you can find your purpose.

Another strength of a highly sensitive person is the ability to see past physical attributions. Sadly, a vast majority of this generation cannot discuss matters of complexity. The media offers a self-absorbing filter of behavior that many young people now try to emulate. As a highly sensitive person, you seek virtue and emphasize the soul as opposed to vanity. You can have genuine relationships with others because you don't emphasize the outward appearance or social status of others.

Your Intuition is Strong

Humans are born with instincts that assist them in fulfilling specific needs. Living as a highly sensitive person, you intuitive abilities are spot on. You are able to understand how individuals operate which can, in turn, guide your behavior. In addition, you know what is right for you and what isn't. When you become confident in your intuitive abilities, you will then learn to do what is best for you without relying heavily on the appraisal of others. This is a unique gift that gives you power and strength.

Understand Your Strengths

Begin to view everything you previously viewed as a detriment as something of value. It's important to create your own worldview and stand by it. Simply because the majority of individuals enjoy large crowds, this does not mean you are meant to do so. Rewire your brain to view your interests as the norm, and do not allow others preferences to shape yours. If certain movies affect you, have confidence in being able to express that.

Your sensitives make you unique and precious. Everyone on this earth has something different that molds their actions. Why should yours be viewed as weak and others as strong? Your insight gives you the opportunity to interact with the human soul on a complex level. Sure, small talk may be beneficial for passing the time, but does it have a purpose? Since you enjoy meaningful discussions, you can express a level of knowledge that is foreign to the majority. Your complexities make you smarter, more knowledgeable, and interesting. Never be ashamed of these qualities.

In addition, being highly sensitive, you can express yourself through creative outlets. Utilize those skills as something that sets you apart from everyone else. You find joy in the creative process and can create brilliance from something you love. How many people can truly say they have hobbies or outlets that give them fulfillment? You can seek your happiness by simply walking outside of your door. Embrace what nature gives you and understand that that in itself is a strength. Embrace your creativities and turn your emotions into innovation.

Your Mission is Unique

Highly sensitive people have the unique inner insight into their mission. They have goals, a meaning, and a purpose that they seek to fulfill. They focus on the betterment of society which is something rare. Many people spend their entire lives attempting to find their meaning; their purpose. They spend countless hours and dollars trying to fill a missing hole in their life. As an Empath, you have your intuition to guide you. You have a strong sense that assists you in making decisions. This could save you from investing time in dangerous individuals or engaging in harmful activities. Unfortunately, this lack of intuition has led some down a path of destruction. Never ignore that intuition in a situation to please others. You have a special gift that is also a safeguard.

You Have Appreciation for Emotions and Nature

There is a beauty in possessing a strong connection with nature and understanding the needs of the earth. The lack of appreciation in this modern world is frightening. The attempt to destroy the earth for capital gain is killing the future. As a highly sensitive person, you understand the importance surrounding appreciation.

In fact, lacking appreciation is a quality of evil pride that rests on entitlement. As an Empath, you possess a humility that many lacks. This humility is incredible and a sign of inner confidence. There is a certain peace that comes from spending time in nature and a certain energy that only Empaths and highly sensitive people benefit from. Understand that strength and take pride in it. The earth is a sacred force that needs more compassion as humans seek to destroy it every day.

You Are a Seeker

Highly sensitive people enjoy meaning. They seek purpose and balance. This often comes with pursuing knowledge through various means. Your predisposition to understanding means you enjoy reading, guidance, and research. In addition, museums and monuments allow you the opportunity to feel the past in a way others cannot. You have an appreciation for the past philanthropy of others, and that appreciation guides your present actions.

One Empath shares being moved to tears when visiting certain national monuments in Washing D.C. The overwhelming appreciation for the sacrifices of past men and women moved her to apply those principles of diligence and care into her daily life. Embrace your knowledge and never be fearful to discuss them with others. You will likely be drawn to similar people who will inspire you as well. Keep your seeker tendencies and continue to pursue enlightenment. In addition, you are able to create meaningful relationships with others because you seek to understand them. You can discuss complex matters, and that helps you to ask inquiring questions to get to know the inner person really. Your goal is to break shallowness with meaning.

Your Soul is Genuine

Unlike the running theme of narcissism, you genuinely care about the future of others. When making relationships, many people focus on what they can get from a person as opposed to developing a solid relationship. As an Empath, your primary goal is to make a connection. You genuinely care about how others feel, you are conscientious, and you strive to be a listening ear.

People confide in you for a specific reason, and your trustworthiness shines. In addition, you emphasize being polite and considerate. This greatly impacts your interpersonal relationships as people know you genuinely care about every aspect of life. The current society is solely focused on a *"me first"* attitude, which disregards praising others. However, you genuinely love seeing others find success, and you feel their happiness with them.

You Really Feel

In a world where so many people have to rely on outward sources to feel something, you have the unique ability to actually feel excitement, happiness, and bliss in its rawest form. Your high connection to emotions is beautiful because you genuinely have fun! Often, many attribute emotions to something negative. However, the emphasis on positive emotions is rarely recognized. As a highly sensitive person, the highs you experience are remarkable in that that you actually feel the complexities of happiness. Your excitement is genuine which is an attractive quality. You wholeheartedly enjoy the achievements of others without jealousy.

Empaths Are an Asset to the Workplace

Sensitivity in the workplace has been frowned upon previously. With many corporations priding themselves on a cut-throat environment, it seems as if an Empath wouldn't survive. Contrary to the popular ideal, highly sensitive people make for amazing employees. They strive to do their best with a performance which impacts productivity. By fearing inadequacy, a healthy work ethic enables them to accomplish tasks at an optimal level.

In addition, being able to tune into the emotions of others and the work environment, they are key to assisting with raising office morale. Many Empathic people find careers in human resources because they are so efficient at solving problems and increasing workplace happiness. They can communicate concerns effectively, and their love for understanding makes them ideal for projects and presentations.

You Thrive in Solitude

Co-dependency is a harmful trait that can block growth. Being highly sensitive, you find great joy in spending time with yourself. In fact, it recharges you. You do not need a surplus of individuals to feel fulfilled. The beauty of being content with your own company is that you are truly never alone. There is a universe of interests that live within your mind. You can enjoy the simple pleasures of life and actually benefit from your imagination.

The strengths as mentioned above merely scratch the surface in comparison to the many talents, and personality traits unique to highly sensitive people. Highly sensitive people find great success in their careers, interpersonal relationships, and family life due to their intuitive nature. The key to owning these strengths is repositioning your current definition of sensitivity and expressing it head on. You can allow the opinions of others to shape how you feel about yourself. Or, you can find strength in what makes you unique and embrace it. Analyze what makes you unique, and soon you will display the warrior-like demeanor you are capable of displaying.

Conclusion

So, you've finished this book, and now you're balanced, energized, and ready to take on the world! The sole purpose of this book is to provide sound advice for people who are natural givers. Highly sensitive people are more than just bags of emotions. They are kind-hearted individuals who feel deeply and are in tune with the emotions of others. If you are a highly sensitive person, and you are still struggling with finding your strengths, perhaps the following integrative and creative projects will assist you with self-exploration. Try to implement these into your daily life so you can visually see your previous weakness turn into a useful source of strength.

Creative Writing Exploration Prompts

Creative writing is an excellent way to turn your weaknesses into strengths. You're the hero of your story, and the perception of your weakness is the villain. Carefully develop the plot to reflect the challenges you face daily. Ask yourself, "how am I able to conquer my villain and become the hero of my own story?" "Who is my support system?" Questions such as these will help to create the ambiance of your narrative and promote self-exploration. Soon, you will be effective in conquering your inner villain and turning it into a valuable gem.

Self-portraits that Encourage Discovery

Do you have a mental image of your sensitivities? Do your trigger points seem to be as massive as an evil monster? Paint a picture of all the aspects of your personality that you wish to work on. Purge those emotional feelings of self-doubt and make your intuition the star. By doing so, you will be able to face your insecurities head-on and develop a stronger trust in your intuitive abilities.

In addition to seeking creative outlets, make having fun the primary focus of your life. Often, highly sensitive people allow the perils of the world and others to dampen their mood. You cannot change your gift, but you can learn to manage it and keep it in its proper place. Despite feeling overwhelmed, take breaks so you can enjoy the merits of life. Do everything you can to restore your energy so that enjoyment inside all of your social settings is practical.

Seek out the best in others, even when your intuition is telling you otherwise. Remember, to remain strong in your intuition, and make decisions that are accurate for you. By doing so, your life will be filled with an immense joy that only comes from developing inner strength. We hope through reading this discourse, you have the power to find strength in your sensitivities.

Finally, thank you for making it through to the end of *Empath: Understanding Your Gift, Protecting your Energy and Finding Peace in a Chaotic World*. Let's hope it was informative and able to provide you with all of the tools you need to achieve your goals whatever they may be.

The next step is to implement all of the tips of the book into your daily life and encourage others to purchase this book as well! By doing so, hopefully, you will gain a better understanding of yourself in addition to advocating for the rights highly sensitive people.

References

Dallenbach, Karl M.; **Bentley**, Madison; **Garrigues**, Edwin; **Washburn**, Margaret Floy. (1910). The American Journal of Psychology p.448

The Atlantic. (2015). Association for Psychological Science. The Atlantic-A Short History of Empathy. Available at: https://www.theatlantic.com/health/archive/2015/10/a-short-history-of-Empathy/409912/

Elert, Glenn. (2018). The Physics Hypertext Book. Available at: https://physics.info/

Oschman, Nora; **Oschman**, Jim. (2018). Reiki News Articles. The International Center for Reiki Training. Science Measures the Human Energy Field. Available at: http://www.reiki.org/reikinews/sciencemeasures.htm

Bergland, Christopher. (2013): The Neuroscience of Empathy. Psychology Today. Available at: https://www.psychologytoday.com/intl/blog/the-athletes-way/201310/the-neuroscience-Empathy

Orloff, Judith. (2017). Psychology Today. The Science behind Empathy and Empaths. Available at: https://www.psychologytoday.com/intl/blog/the-Empaths-survival-guide/201703/the-science-behind-Empathy-and-Empaths

Body Quirks. (2012). Total Body Solutions. Must Have Tools for the Empath. Available at: http://www.bodyquirks.com/2012/02/7-must-have-tools-for-the-Empath/

The Mind Unleashed. (2013). Tree Hugging Now Scientifically Validated. Available at: https://themindunleashed.com/2013/07/tree-hugging-now-scientifically.html

The Mind Unleashed. (2013). 30 Traits of the Empath. Available at: https://themindunleashed.com/2013/10/30-traits-of-Empath.html

Thor, Erik. (2018). Personal Growth Influencer. The Hidden Issues of the Empath. Available at: https://www.erikthor.com/2017/01/09/issues-of-the-Empath/

Van Kimmenade, Caroline. (2011). The Happy Sensitive. Essential Boundaries for HSPs and Empaths. Available at: https://thehappysensitive.com/essential-boundaries-for-hsps-and-Empaths-keeping-track-of-our-own-well-being/

Leonard, Laurie. (2017). CURE. Cancer Updates, Research & Education. The Healing Arts in Palliative Care. Available at: https://www.curetoday.com/publications/cure/

2017/fall-2017/the-healing-arts-in-palliative-care

Miro. (2013). Warrior Poets Wisdom: *Empath*. Available at: https://warriorpoetwisdom.com/2012/07/25/Empaths/

Castro, Joseph. (2012). Live Science. How A Mother's Love Changes A Child's Brain. Available at: https://www.livescience.com/18196-maternal-support-child-brain.html

Harwin, Cliff. (2013). Highly Sensitive Thoughts: I'm Proud to be a perfectionist! Available at: http://highlysensitivethoughts.com/2013/06/10/uncategorized/highly-sensitive-people-im-proud-to-be-a-perfectionist/

About the Author

Jessica Greiner is an author and a mother of two daughters. With a degree in Psychology, Jessica is passionate about helping people develop their inner emotional, psychic and sensual life. She believes that by understanding our brain and our emotions, why we do what we do, we are better equipped to deal with the various challenges we encounter in life.

Jessica writes books that are easy to understand and shares strategies that can be easily applied to everyone's day to day life. She has always been fascinated with the way people interact with others and the rest of the world. This interest has led her to the life of learning several factors affecting human interactions. Moreover, she continually works on expanding her knowledge by attending seminars and networking with other professionals.

When not writing, Jessica enjoys spending time horseback riding with her daughters or relaxing at the lake with her husband.